For Mirte and Seppe, who help me discover the world with fresh eyes every day.
–J.L.

MISSION
TO THE BOTTOM OF
THE SEA

Written by Jan Leyssens
Illustrated by Joachim Sneyers

Clavis

NEW YORK

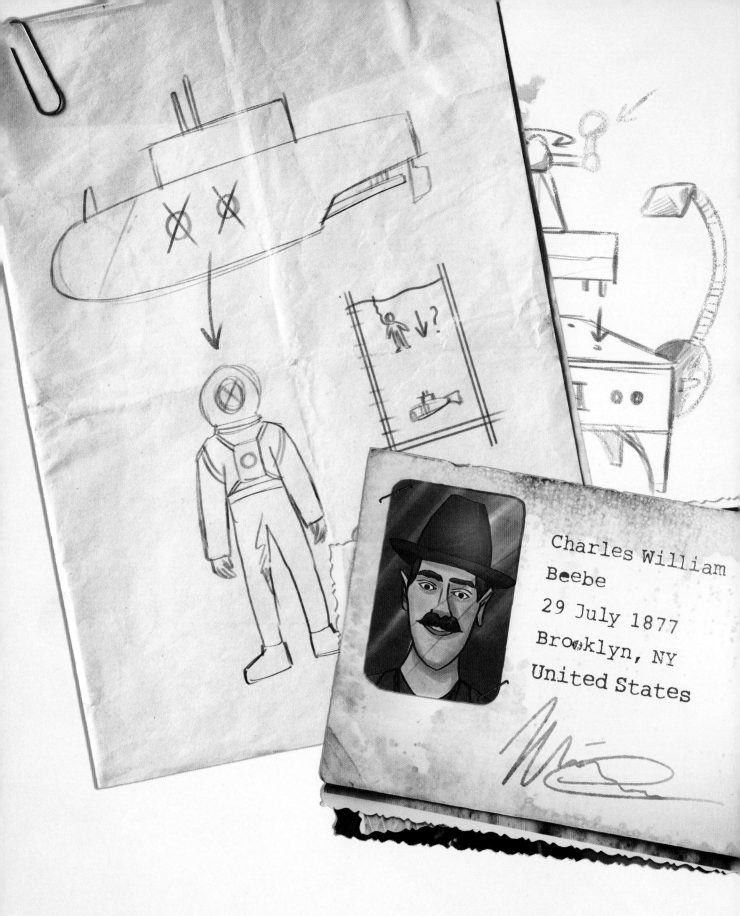

Charles William
Beebe
29 July 1877
Brooklyn, NY
United States

Meet William Beebe, an American scientist, explorer, and nature lover. He lived in the early 1900s and spent many days exploring the coral reefs in Bermuda. He wanted to dive deeper, but the diving suit he wore wasn't resistant to the pressure of deeper water. So he had to come up with a new way to descend further into the sea . . .

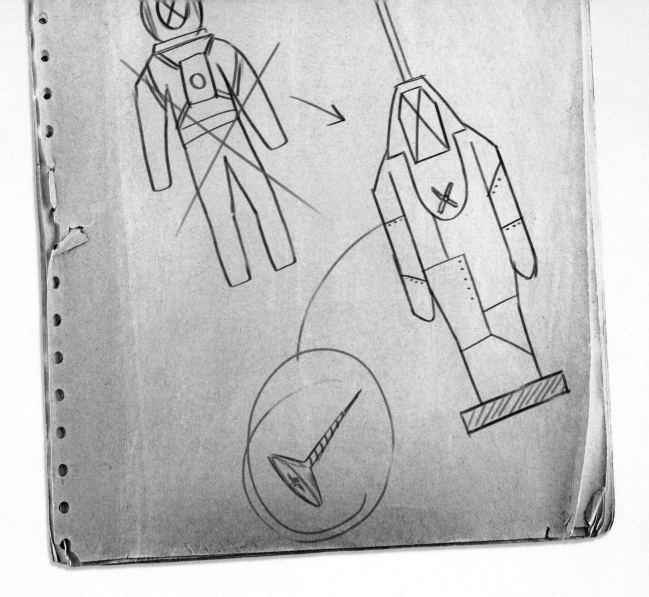

The depths that William wanted to explore were unreachable with an ordinary diving suit. Others used steel suits for deep dives, but William was worried that this kind of suit would be too dangerous. He realized that what he needed was a submarine. So William put an ad in the newspaper.

WANTED

A NEW KIND OF SUBMARINE
THAT CAN GO MUCH DEEPER THAN THE CURRENT ONES.

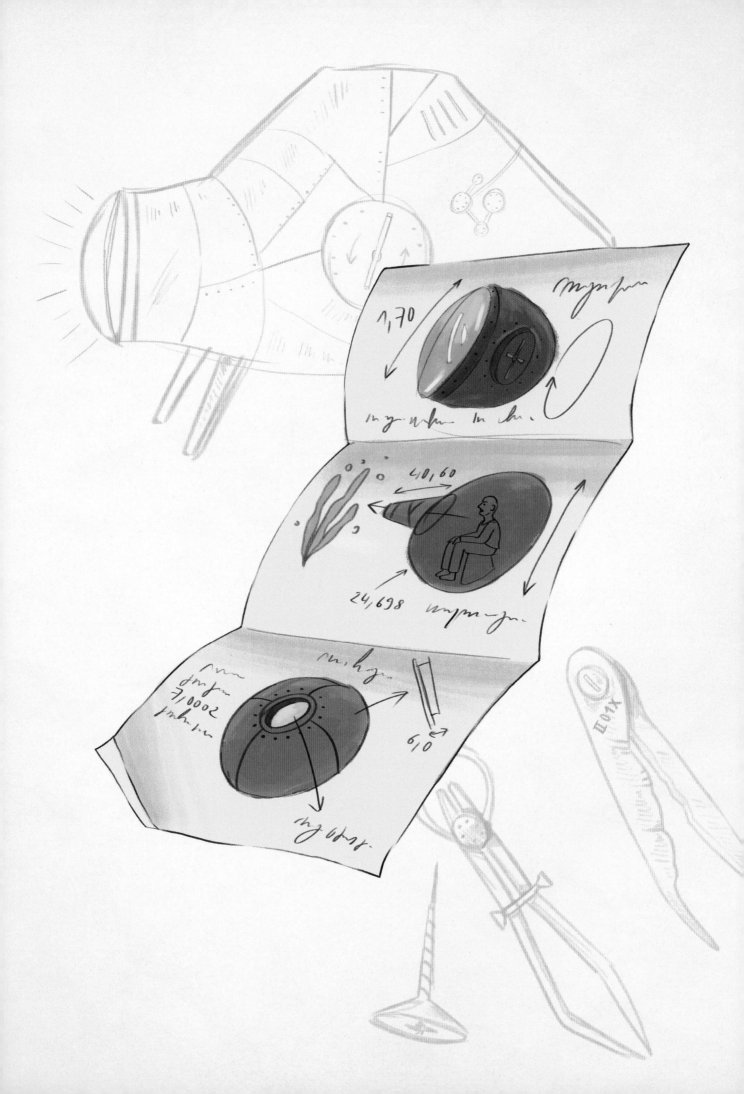

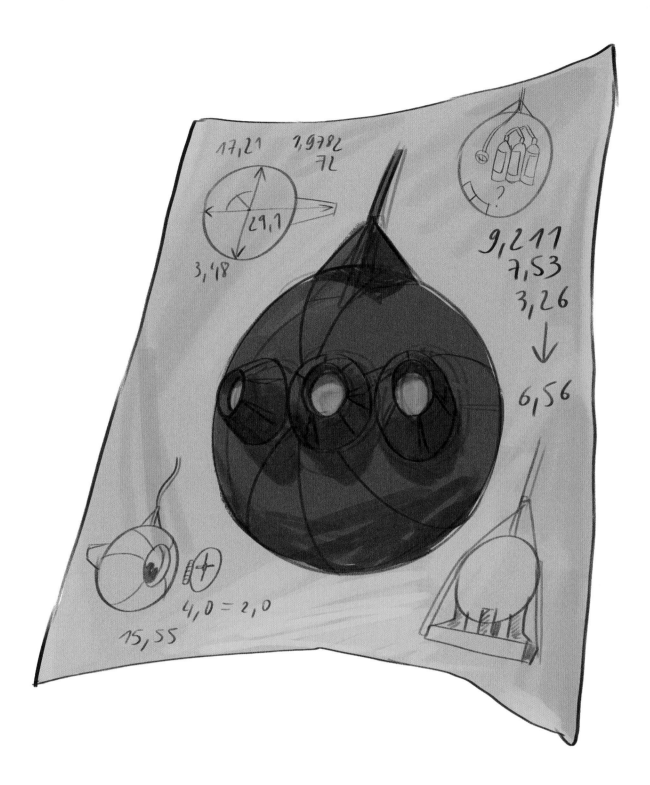

The ad was seen by Otis Barton, an engineer who was also curious about the depths of the sea. He wrote William a letter including his design for a submarine that could go deeper than traditional subs. Otis offered to build the submarine for William, but only on one condition. He wanted to go on an expedition with him!

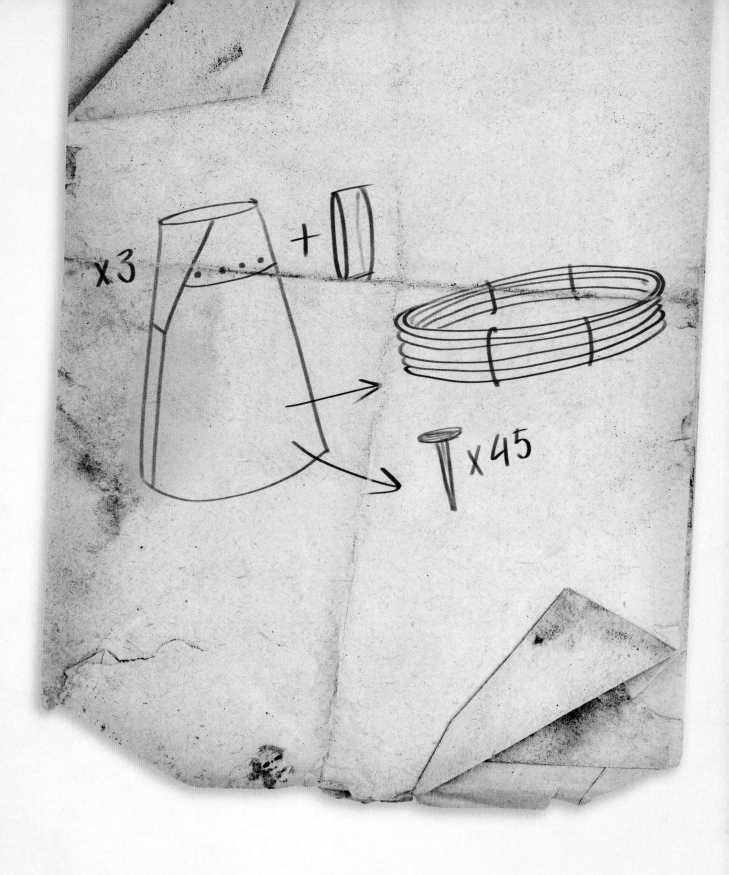

Otis's design was a large steel sphere on a cable that could be lowered into the sea from a ship. The windows in the sphere were almost three inches thick and would allow the researchers a great view of the waters around them. William called the vessel the Bathysphere.

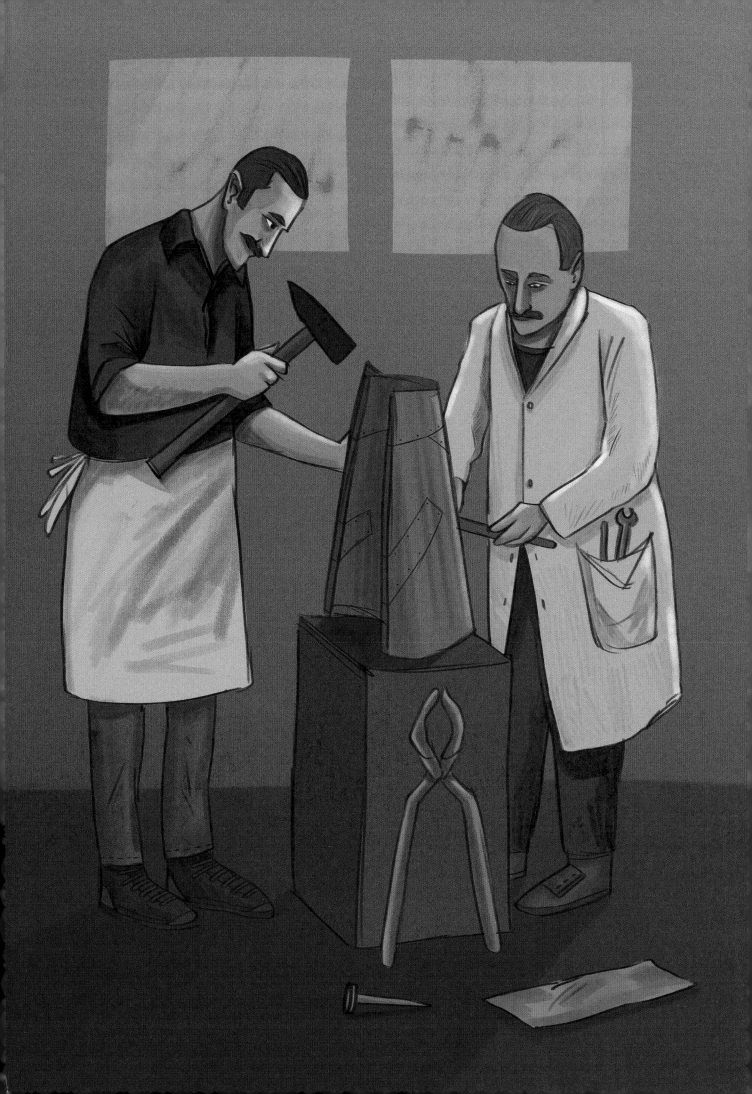

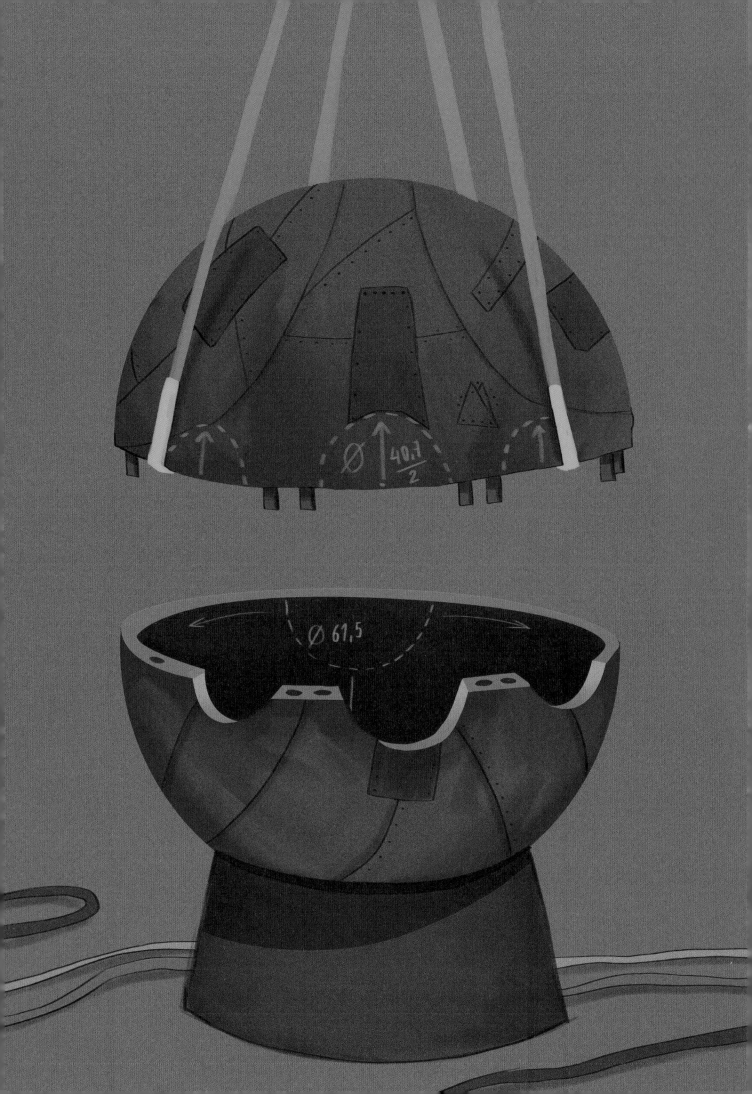

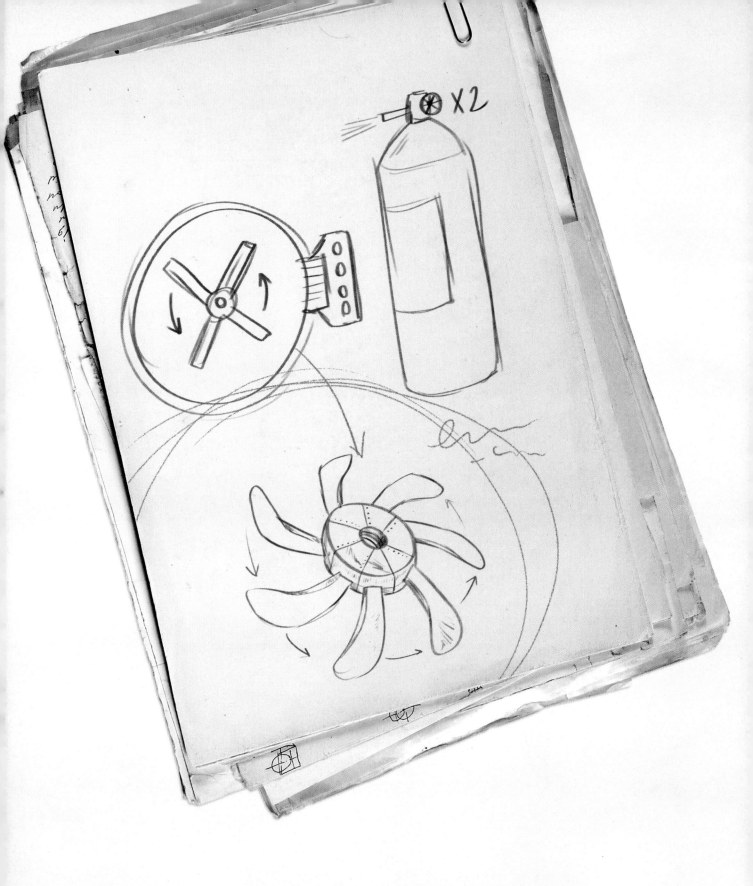

The Bathysphere was small—only about five feet wide. But it was just big enough for the two men. And it was filled with everything they needed, including two oxygen tanks, a depth gauge, and lamps to shine light in the darkness. They knew it could be terrifyingly dark in the deep sea . . .

William and Otis knew better than to go directly into deep water with the Bathysphere. First they tested the design for leaks and other problems in shallow water. Then they tested it without passengers in deep water. Finally, William and Otis thought it was time to descend to the deep sea. They were filled with anticipation when they stepped into the Bathysphere . . .

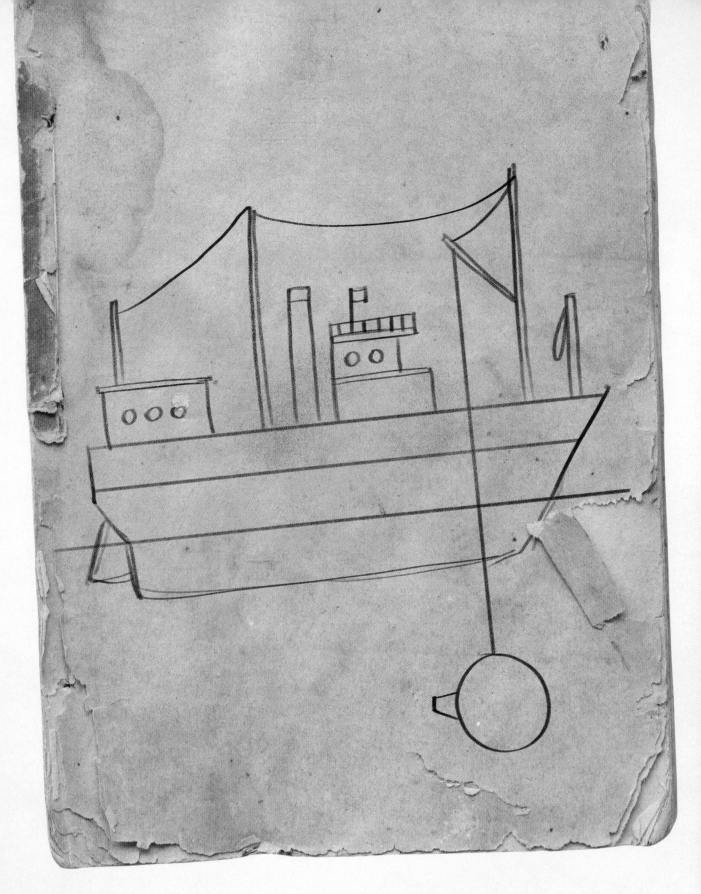

. . . and with success! William and Otis dropped to a depth of almost three thousand feet in the sea. That was six times deeper than anyone had ever been before! People were curious about their expeditions to the underwater world. One day they gave a radio interview from the Bathysphere while they were deep in the ocean. The waves were so wild that Otis got seasick in the middle of the broadcast. Still, he continued the interview.

In the deep sea, William and Otis discovered marine animals no one had ever seen before. Since there were no cameras in those days, they used a kind of telephone line to report what they saw to people in the boat above them.

One of those people at the surface was Else Bostelmann, an illustrator who sketched everything the men described from the Bathysphere. Her drawings were sent to newspapers and magazines around the world. People were amazed by these underwater discoveries.

The expeditions of William and Otis were a great inspiration for scientists who also wanted to explore the deep sea. Years later, when new, better submarines filled with modern photographic equipment were developed, it became clear that the animals that William and Otis discovered really do exist.

The Bathysphere was used for only four years. Yet we learned a great deal from the expeditions that William and Otis made in their little submarine. Today you can admire the Bathysphere at the New York Aquarium.